Test your

Financial
Awareness

JOHN HODGSON

Series editors: GARETH LEWIS & GENE CROZIER

Hodder & Stoughton

A MEMBER OF THE HODDER HEADLINE GROUP

Orders: please contact Bookpoint Ltd, 39 Milton Park, Abingdon, Oxon OX14
4TD. Telephone: (44) 01235 400414, Fax: (44) 01235 400454. Lines are open from
9.00 – 6.00, Monday to Saturday, with a 24 hour message answering service.
Email address: orders@bookpoint.co.uk

British Library Cataloguing in Publication Data
A catalogue record for this title is available from The British Library

ISBN 0 340 782870

First published 2000
Impression number   10 9 8 7 6 5 4 3 2 1
Year   2004 2003 2002 2001 2000

Copyright © 2000 John Hodgson

Typeset by Fakenham Photosetting Limited, Fakenham, Norfolk.
Printed in Great Britain for Hodder & Stoughton Education, a division of
Hodder Headline Plc, 338 Euston Road, London NW1 3BH by Cox & Wyman
Ltd, Reading, Berkshire.

in *the Institute*
of Management

The Institute of Management (IM) is the leading organisation for professional management. Its purpose is to promote the art and science of management in every sector and at every level, through research, education, training and development, and representation of members' views on management issues.

This series is commissioned by IM Enterprises Limited, a subsidiary of the Institute of Management, providing commercial services.

Management House,
Cottingham Road,
Corby,
Northants NN17 1TT
Tel: 01536 204222;
Fax: 01536 201651
Website: http://www.inst-mgt.org.uk

Registered in England no 3834492
Registered office: 2 Savoy Court, Strand,
London WC2R 0EZ

Contents

Foreword

There are so many books on the market on this particular subject that it gives me pleasure to commend this one.

I have been teaching this subject for some ten years now, and the main barriers I have found are a basic fear of figures, and the fear of looking foolish by asking questions.

There is no doubt in my mind that figures that are not questioned are figures that will eventually become incorrect; and who better to question them than the managers that have done the business in the period in question?

This book's main virtue is that it attempts to keep its subject as simple as possible. The subject has unfortunately been clouded by jargon and legalese, and any attempt to demystify it can only be applauded. This book will help to lift the fog.

This book looks at the subject from a manager's point of view, and does not bog the reader down in unnecessary technical details that they do not need for a simple understanding of financial reports. True, it is basic, but that is what many managers crave. When they have fully grasped the basics, they are able to move at greater speed, and are more fully aware of, and committed to, the financial goals of their organisation.

As business becomes more and more competitive, companies become more and more financially obsessed. Financial targets and goals are increasing in importance, with managers' remuneration often closely linked to financial performance.

Companies are ruled by financial performance, and it is an imperative for managers to understand their company's finances, and question and use financial reports for better decision taking.

Anthony Parmiter FCA

Introduction

This book will help you become a more effective manager by improving your understanding of basic business finance and will help you make better business decisions based on financial input.

Competitive advantage is gained when an organisation delivers products and services of superior quality and value. The survival of a commercial organisation ultimately demands that customer satisfaction be achieved at a profit. Every person who is in a position to determine the way in which assets are utilised, sales revenues earned or expenses incurred, influences profit. For this reason, financial knowledge and commercial understanding are acknowledged as core competencies for managers and team leaders alike.

This book is for non-financial managers who would like to have greater confidence in reading financial reports and discussing financial issues. The book has been written not by an accountant, but by someone who moved through the ranks of a large multi-national organisation. He discovered that the higher up the ladder he went, the less he understood about the business in financial terms. At times he thought he was alone. Some years later, and after making numerous mistakes due to ignorance, he discovered he was not alone after all. As it turned out most of his colleagues who sat through the same meetings had also suffered in silence.

In front of them were documents headed *Monthly Profit and Loss*, *Contribution Report* and *Budget Variance Analysis*.

Nobody it seems was prepared to raise their hand and say, 'Sorry, I really don't understand what this means.' The financial controller would discuss the documents. To most it sounded like a foreign language. Managers sat in silence and hoped that a furrowed brow and concerned expression was enough to convey understanding.

Questioning the figures was deemed unnecessary. On the rare occasions they were challenged, the answers often led to more confusion and even more quizzical looks. The only protection was the financial controller knew as much about selling as they knew about finance. They would regularly convince him that the only way to move stock was to: 'offer more discount', 'have another promotion', 'increase the advertising budget', but the favourite was 'give the customers extra credit'.

For those in sales, performance was measured in terms of units sold, sales volume and market share. They were blissfully unaware of the connection between stock and return on investment or of overstocking and cost of sales. Ignorance, it seems, was bliss. Eventually the company was purchased by a foreign competitor and today thrives as a global leader in consumer products.

Today, the speed and ease with which financial information is downloaded to everybody's desktop has increased the necessity for more managers to have the ability to interpret financial statements. This book is for all those new and aspiring managers who feel the need to improve their understanding of the language and the numbers.

Pitfalls of not understanding the language and the numbers

- You may be overlooked when it comes to promotion.
- You may, through ignorance, make costly mistakes.
- You may not know how you and your team affect the bottom line (could you even explain what the bottom line is if asked to do so?).
- You may not be able to understand your company's financial reports.
- You may feel isolated or embarrassed in meetings when financial matters are discussed.
- You may become a costly overhead that needs to be eliminated.

Overview

The aim of this book is to introduce the reader to the most commonly used financial terms in business today. The style is basic and readily understandable. It uses easy to follow examples and the reader has the chance to test his/her knowledge at regular intervals throughout the book.

Apart from computers and I.T. no other subject than finance contains as many acronyms and jargon. This book will take you on a journey from basic principles to more complex financial measures. It explodes the myth that finance is difficult to understand or that a university degree is needed to read a set of accounts.

Today, more and more people, from the most junior, to the most senior, are expected to make decisions based on financial input. This book will help you understand the most commonly used financial reports and the inescapable jargon that accompanies them. You may feel tempted to say, 'This all sounds a bit basic to me. I think I'm already at a higher level.' Fine, that may well be the case. If so you may know a colleague who would benefit and decide to pass the book to them. But, before you do why not invest a few minutes of your time to test yourself with the introductory test on the next page.

A score of 80% + suggests you have a good understanding, but have a few gaps in your knowledge. The book will certainly help strengthen your understanding. Should your score be less than 80%, the answers are literally in your hands. Good luck.

Author's note
As you work your way through the book, you will encounter a number of acronyms and financial terms. When they are introduced for the first time they will be explained.

Introductory test

The test is a list of 20 statements. Each statement is either true or false. Place a tick against those statements which you believe are true, and an 'x' against those statements which are false. If you don't know the answer move to the next statement. Don't feel bad if you don't know any of them. Try to avoid the temptation of skipping to the answers. You will never know your true starting point and will lose the reference point when you come to do it for the second time.

On completion of the test check your answers with those on pages 13–15. Add the number of correct answers and multiply the total by 5 to give your starting percentage. This is a self-assessment that nobody else needs to know. You should refer to it when you've completed the final test to see how far you've progressed.

Don't worry if your score is low. The lower it is the more you have to gain by reading the book.

?

Test Yourself

Self-assessment – financial awareness

Please indicate whether the following statements are true or false

	T	F
1. The top line of the profit and loss account shows the owners' equity	☐	☐
2. Working capital is the same as net assets	☐	☐
3. The balance sheet is sometimes referred to as a financial snapshot of a business	☐	☐
4. The assets of a business are funded by debtors	☐	☐
5. Cost of sales is equal to opening stock plus purchases less closing stock	☐	☐
6. Gross margin is usually expressed as gross profit divided by sales multiplied by 100	☐	☐
7. A current ratio of 1:1 is considered healthy	☐	☐
8. Current liabilities usually include terms such as stock, debtors and cash	☐	☐
9. Stock is a current asset and is shown on the profit and loss account	☐	☐

10. Net margin is the same as return on sales ☐ ☐

11. Return on Investment (R.O.I.) is calculated by dividing gross profit by sales multiplied by 100 ☐ ☐

12. Retained profit shown on the profit and loss account will result in a change in owners' equity on the balance sheet. ☐ ☐

13. Reducing variable costs has the effect of increasing the contribution to fixed costs and profit ☐ ☐

14. Return on net assets can be calculated from the balance sheet alone ☐ ☐

15. Sales less working capital equals net current assets ☐ ☐

16. Contribution is gross profit less variable costs ☐ ☐

17. The bottom line is another name for working capital ☐ ☐

18. A cash flow forecast enables a company to estimate its projected receipts and expenditures ☐ ☐

19. Raw materials are usually classified as variable costs ☐ ☐

20. The debtors' collection period indicates how quickly the debtors of a business are paying for their credit purchases ☐ ☐

Now check your answers with those on the following pages.

Add up the total _correct_ answers multiply by 5 = ... %

Answers to Introductory test

Next to each answer are a few words of explanation. You are not expected to fully understand all of the answers at this stage. They will become clear as you work your way through the book.

By the time you've finished the book you can expect to complete the quiz with 100% accuracy and complete understanding:

1. **False**   The top line of the profit and loss account is Sales/Turnover/Revenue/Income.
2. **False**   Working capital is the same as net *current* assets.
3. **True**   The balance sheet is compiled at the end of an accounting period and shows the assets and liabilities at a 'frozen' moment in time.
4. **False**   Assets of a business are made up of fixed and current assets. Current assets include stock, *debtors* and cash.
5. **True**   Cost of sales formula is fully explained in a later chapter.
6. **True**   Gross margin is gross profit expressed as a percentage of sales.
7. **False**   The current ratio is a liquidity ratio and shows the relationship between the amount of money a company *owes* in the short-term (current liabilities) and how much it *owns* in the short-term (current assets). A ratio of 2:1 is considered healthy.
8. **False**   Stock, debtors and cash are current assets, not current liabilities.

9. **False**   Stock *is* a current asset but it is found on the balance sheet.

10. **True**   They are interchangeable names. In both cases the formula is net profit divided by sales multiplied by 100. In other words net profit expressed as a percentage of sales.

11. **False**   The formula for Return on Investment is net profit divided by total assets multiplied by 100.

12. **True**   Retained profit increases accumulated profit which goes to the balance sheet as reserves and is added to share capital. This increases owners' equity.

13. **True**   The formula for contribution is sales less variable costs. Therefore, any reduction in variable costs will increase contribution. (In case you're wondering, contribution in this context goes towards fixed costs and thereafter profit.)

14. **False**   You need the profit and loss account for the net profit and the balance sheet for the net assets.

15. **False**   To begin with, working capital and net current assets are the same. Next, whereas sales is the top line of the profit and loss account, working capital or net current assets is a line on the balance sheet. Deducting one from the other serves no purpose. The calculation has no value whatsoever.

16. **False**   Contribution is *sales* less variable costs.

17. **False**   The bottom line refers to net profit before interest and tax.
18. **True**   The cashflow statement is the budget expressed in terms of cash flowing into the business and cash flowing out.
19. **True**   Any cost that varies in direct proportion to output is a variable cost.
20. **True**   Debtors collection period or debtor days is an indication of the number of days it is taking for the company to collect money due.

All formulae referred to in this quiz are fully explained in later chapters. Now, let's begin to explore the world of business finance.

Profit and loss account: Part 1

Every company in every industry aims to make a profit. Profit is necessary for growth and profit is achieved when total income (sales) exceeds total operating costs, otherwise known as expenses.

Example

	Company A £	Company B £
Sales	1000	1000
Total operating costs	900	1050
Net profit/loss	100	(50)

In this example Company A's income from sales is more than total operating costs, so we say that Company A has made a profit of £100.

Company B also has sales of £1000 but their total operating costs are £1050. Company B has made a loss of £50. Note that the loss is shown in brackets. This is a simple profit and loss account. It shows total sales, total costs and the difference between the two. The period it covers is called an accounting period. It may be for a day, a week, a month, a quarter or a full year. From this point forward most of the financial documents we will be dealing with will be for a 12 month accounting period. The amounts shown on a profit and loss account under the heading 'sales' are exclusive of VAT.

As you proceed through the book you will see profit and loss accounts containing many more lines of information.

You'll see various ways of breaking down costs plus different types of profit. For now just remember that sales minus total cost equals profit, and that a company needs to make profit to survive.

Sales

The top line of the profit and loss account shows the value of sales for the period. The profit and loss account may begin 'Profit and loss account for year ended 31st December 1999', or some other date.

Not all organisations use sales for the top line. While 'sales' is the most commonly used word there are alternatives:

- turnover
- revenue
- income
- fees

In some organisations the profit and loss account is known as the income statement or revenue statement. Charities in particular use the term income statement. The top line of the income statement will read 'Income', followed by a list of operating costs. Where you expect to see the word 'Profit' you'll see 'Surplus'. Where you expect to see 'Loss' you'll see 'Deficit'. Sales or income, profit or surplus, the same rules apply. When total costs exceed sales or income, profit or surplus becomes loss or deficit.

It's hardly surprising that non-accountants sometimes get confused with the language. We've already seen that sales is sometimes called turnover or income and that the profit and loss account is sometimes called the income or revenue statement. Similarly, you will encounter alternative names for net profit.

Here are some examples:

- operating profit
- trading profit
- net profit before tax
- pre-tax profit
- earnings
- bottom line

For consistency, we will use sales and net profit whenever we refer to these two lines on the profit and loss account.

Later in the book you will see that a profit and loss account contains much more information than just sales, costs and profit. You'll see details of interest charges, tax payments, dividends and retained profit. Why then is net profit described as the bottom line when clearly it isn't?

There are good reasons. It's a fact that everybody in an organisation influences the bottom line. That's because everybody in an organisation has varying degrees of influence over sales and costs. The chairman or proprietor may decide to change pricing policy – that would almost certainly have an effect on the bottom line. The manual worker may use excessive amounts of time or raw material to complete a job – that too has a direct impact on the bottom line.

However, interest charges, corporation tax and dividends are outside the remit of most employees. That is why for all

employees the world over net profit is referred to as the
bottom line, being the point on the profit and loss account
where their influence generally comes to a halt.

NOTE
The more accurate term for bottom line is Net Profit before
Interest and Tax which may be shortened to NPBIT.

Simple profit and loss account

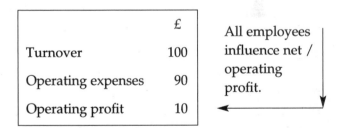

	£
Sales	100
Total costs	90
Net profit	10

All employees
influence the
bottom line

The same profit and loss account using alternative words

	£
Turnover	100
Operating expenses	90
Operating profit	10

All employees
influence net /
operating
profit.

Costs or expenses?

Again we have a choice. Whether a company chooses to
label certain items as costs or expenses is down to them.
There's no hard and fast rule.

If a business sees costs/expenses rise and there is no

increase in sales to compensate, profit will be smaller. In that respect one golden rule worth noting is: 'higher costs mean lower profit.'

Diagram of a profit and loss account

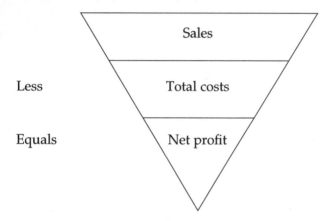

Less   Sales / Total costs

Equals   Net profit

Effect on profit from changes in sales or costs.

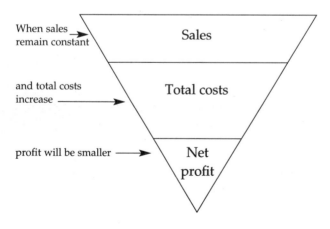

When sales remain constant → Sales

and total costs increase → Total costs

profit will be smaller → Net profit

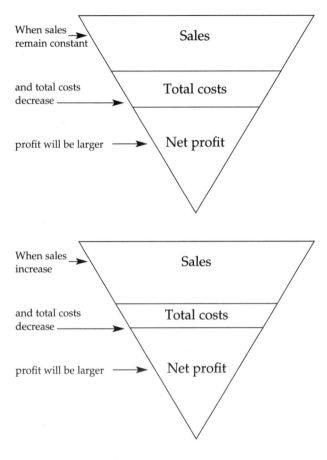

A key financial measure which we calculate from the sales and net profit figures on the profit and loss account is: **return on sales (ROS).**

The return on sales ratio is used to express profit as a percentage of sales. It is one of the most commonly used financial measures. It is also known as **net margin**.

The use of the return on sales equation is widely used in

retail, in manufacturing, in the service sector and in the private sector. It's quick and simple to calculate and is used to highlight movements in sales and costs.

Below are figures extracted from the profit and loss account of three companies competing in the same market.

Extract from profit and loss accounts for period ended 31st December 1997

	A £	B £	C £
Sales	1000	1400	1175
Total costs	750	1100	900
Net profit	250	300	275

? Test Yourself

First, just study the numbers. *Do not* attempt to calculate return on sales. Consider what the numbers tell you about the financial performance of each company.

(Circle as appropriate)

Which company made the most profit?	A	B	C
Which company has the highest sales?	A	B	C
Which company has the lowest costs?	A	B	C

What else do the figures tell you?

You probably said that:

- Company B made the most profit – £300 compared to £250 and £275.

- Company B has the highest sales – £1400 compared to £1000 and £1175.
- Company A has the lowest sales, lowest costs and lowest profit.
- Company C falls in the middle as far as sales, cost and profit are concerned.

It's unlikely that you were able to add much more without calculating return on sales. As you would have noted, Company B made the *most profit*. That is not to say that Company B was the *most profitable*.

It's important to understand the distinction between profit and profitability. Think of profit as the number of pounds of profit shown on the profit and loss account and profitability as being an indication of sales and cost efficiency.

As you work your way through the book you will find other profitability ratios but at this point we only have a limited amount of information to go on, but we have enough to use the first one in the book, namely return on sales. A company should aim to improve its profitability by monitoring sales and costs using the return on sales formula.

Formula for return on sales/net margin

$$\frac{\text{Net Profit} \times 100}{\text{Sales}} = \%$$

Extract from profit and loss accounts of three companies for period ended 31st December 1997

	A £	B £	C £
Sales	1000	1400	1175
Total costs	750	1100	900
Net profit	250	300	275

?

Test Yourself

Using the information given above calculate the return on sales for each of the three companies.

Company A | Company B | Company C

(Correct answers are shown below)

You now have a meaningful comparison and a different picture begins to emerge.

Before moving on check your answers:

Company A – 25%   Company B – 21.43%   Company C – 23.4%

The company with the lowest sales, lowest costs and lowest profit turns out to be the most profitable. Using the return on sales formula shows us that Company A was the most profitable. True, Company B made the most profit but in terms of return on sales it was out-performed by Company A. 25% ROS for A compared with 21.43% for B.

STOP PRESS

Company B has purchased Company A. The new company is called The AB Company Ltd. Where before the market had three companies in direct competition there are now two. The newly formed AB Company Ltd and the established C Company Ltd.

Market research indicates market growth of 40% over the next three years. With reduced competition both companies decide to widen their range of products. They each decide to go from being a one-product company to having a family of three. In both cases they plan to manufacture products that will appeal to different types of consumer. The products are satellite navigation systems for use in the car and the plan is to distribute them via a network of specialist retailers in the motor accessory trade.

The two companies embark on a programme of research and development and launch new products within weeks of each other. Everything appears to be going to plan, for both companies. Consumers respond well to the range of options. There is a clear link between price and performance. The higher priced products include a micro chip that 'talks' to the motorist, has additional features and improved graphics. The lower priced models have no sound, fewer features and the graphics are less detailed. Both the AB and the C companies step up production in response to trade and consumer reaction.

Two years pass
You are appointed General manager of the AB company and one of your first tasks is to comment on recently published financial results.

The profit and loss accounts for period ended 31st December 1999 reveal:

	Company AB £000's	Company C £000's
Sales	2500	1400
Total operating costs	2250	1250
Net profit	250	250

You decide to compare return on sales.

Company AB   Company C

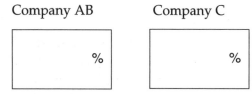

(Calculate the answers before reading on)

You will see that the ROS for the AB Company is 10% and 17.86% for C Company. In both cases, when compared to their respective ROS in 1997, the ROS has fallen.

The AB Company Ltd
The return on sales has gone down from 21.43% in 1997 to 10% in 1999.

The C Company Ltd
The return on sales has gone down from 23.4% in 1997 to 17.86% in 1999.

You've been asked for your initial observations.

? **Test Yourself**

a) What are you able to say with absolute certainty?

b) What additional information would you like to have?

Think about your answers before moving on to the suggestions that follow.

To keep things simple and avoid lots of number crunching ignore the fact that the P & L reports the results in £millions. In this instance use the numbers below. Don't worry about the extra zeros. The percentage and subsequent message will not be affected.

a) What were you able to say with absolute certainty?
That the results for Company AB and Company C reveal: the newly formed AB Company Ltd reported sales of £2500 in 1999 whereas in 1997 sales for the then independent A and B companies were £1000 and £1400 respectively. The consolidated accounts show an overall increase of £100. Company C Ltd has increased its sales from £1175 to £1400, an increase of £225.

The consolidated accounts of the AB Company show profit down from £550 in 1997 to £250 in 1999. For Company C, profit is also down, from £275 in 1997 to £250 in 1999.

Operating costs in the AB Company are £2250. Prior to the purchase they were £750 for Company A and £1100 for Company B. Finally, operating costs for Company C have risen from £900 to £1250.

You were asked to say what the figures allow you to say with absolute certainty. It's obvious that you need a lot more information. The simple sales minus costs equals profit formula is severely lacking in detail.

You were then asked:

b) What additional information would you like to see?
You should be asking to see a breakdown of total costs. It is not possible to add much more without more detailed information. You should ask for details of the cost of sales and operating expenses. By seeing a more detailed profit and loss account with cost of sales included, you will be able to calculate another key financial performance measure known as **gross profit**, and then **gross margin**.

Let's leave the AB and C companies and begin to examine the profit and loss account in more detail. Below is the familiar diagram of a profit and loss account. Note that it includes two more lines of information: one headed cost of sales and the other gross profit.

Cost of sales and gross profit

Profit and loss account

Cost of sales
Cost of sales, otherwise known as cost of goods sold, may
be shortened to COS, or COGS. There is no difference in
their meaning. A profit and loss account showing cost of
sales and gross profit will typically look like this.

Profit and loss account for the year ending 19…..

	£ooo's	
Sales	140	
Cost of sales	(90)	
Gross profit	50	(TOTAL COSTS)
Operating expenses	(40)	
Net profit	10	

In this example, cost of sales and operating expenses are
shown in brackets. This may not always be the case.
Sometimes the negative figure may be preceded by a minus
sign. On other occasions the figures will have neither
brackets nor minus sign. Presentation of the figures is often
a matter of personal choice or may be dictated by computer
software. The important thing to remember with all financial
reporting is the need to be *consistent*. If you decide to use
brackets to highlight negative numbers, fine. If you decide to
use a minus sign, that too is fine. But don't make the mistake
of mixing them up. At best it will lead to confusion. At
worst, a decision risks being made on wrong information.

Notice too that total costs have been divided into cost of
sales and operating expenses. Cost of sales is the cost of
goods 'sold' during the accounting period. It is deducted
from Sales to leave Gross Profit. In a manufacturing
organisation it would typically include:

- Raw materials
- Work-in-Progress (referred to as WIP)
- Finished goods.

In some parts of the world, in America for example, Work-in-Progress may be referred to as Work-in-Process.

Cost of sales may also include the cost of direct labour and the cost of utilities directly associated with the manufacturing process. A chemical processing plant is likely to incur high energy costs and may choose to include a proportion of those costs with cost of sales. A retail organisation would not typically have work-in-progress. A service organisation would not typically report Cost of Sales as a separate item on their profit and loss account, unless their sales included a product component.

In all cases the formula used for calculating Cost of Sales is the same:

Formula for cost of sales

Opening stock + Purchases − Closing stock

Without an increase in sales, any increase in cost of sales will reduce gross profit.

Apart from the items already mentioned such as raw materials, work-in-progress and finished goods, perhaps the one area that has the greatest influence on cost of sales is shrinkage. Most people think of shrinkage as staff and customer theft. It's much more than that, and rarely gets measured. Think of stock damage: goods that go out of style or fashion, goods that go past their sell-by date that have to be reduced to make way for new stock. When this happens the cost of sales goes up by the same amount that the goods are reduced.

Consider this:

A company starts the year with stock of £1,000. The stock may be in raw materials, work-in-progress or finished goods. At each stage it becomes progressively more valuable. This is reflected in the value attached to it.

During the course of the year the company purchases raw materials costing £2,000. Opening stock plus purchases means it had stock valued at £3,000 available for sale. At the end of the year it carried out a stock-take. The year end stock value was £500.

Using the cost of sales formula of opening stock plus purchases less closing stock, the cost of sales figure reported on the profit and loss account is expected to show £2,500.

However, the general manager notices a discrepancy. The year end stock of £500 includes items which he believes will only sell if the price is reduced. A stock re-valuation is requested. Some of the finished goods are imperfect. They failed final test. A decision must be made. Is it better to re-work them and bring them up to standard or reduce the price to make way for new stock?

A closer inspection of stock in the warehouse reveals water damage to some of the packaging. After a brief discussion with the financial controller a decision is taken to reduce the value of year end stock from £500 to £200. The cost of sales figure as reported in the profit and loss account will change.

? ## Test Yourself

Before the decision was made to reduce the value of stock, cost of sales entry was expected to be £2,500. After reducing stock to £200 what is the revised cost of sales?

Answer

Opening stock	+	Purchases	−	Closing stock
£1,000		£2,000		£200

Cost of sales is now £2,800

The need to re-value stock is not at all uncommon. In fact it's quite usual. That is not to say that we should accept it as the norm. The term 'current asset management' springs to mind. It should be the responsibility of everybody in an organisation to do what they can to minimise the need for stock losses and re-valuation. The adjustments made cascade through the profit and loss account and affect almost all of the subsequent financial performance measures. But first, let's concentrate on the next line of the profit and loss account.

Gross profit
Gross profit is the difference between sales and cost of sales. It is from this amount that all other operating costs or expenses must be met. Clearly, anything we do that unnecessarily increases cost of sales, for whatever reason, will reduce gross profit. Conversely, anything we do that reduces the risk or need to write stock down or write stock off will protect gross profit and have a beneficial effect on financial results.

The Really Bright Manufacturing Company Ltd manufactures mobile telephones. Sales for the financial year ended 31st March 2000 were £1,200,000.

Cost of sales was calculated as follows:

Opening stock	£500,000
+	
Purchases	£400,000
–	
Closing stock	£200,000

Cost of Sales = £700,000

The Really Bright Manufacturing Company Ltd
profit and loss account
for year ended 31st March 2000

	£ 000's
Sales	1,200
Cost of sales	700
Gross profit	500
Operating expenses	275
Net profit	225

The company carries out a stock check and takes the decision to reduce the value of closing stock from £200,000 to £50,000 (this information is taken from the Balance Sheet which we cover in depth in a later chapter).

Take a look at the profit and loss account below. For purposes of comparison only we have shown the forecast results under the heading 'Original' and actual results under 'Revised'. See how the entire stock adjustment figure has dropped through to the bottom line. The £150,000 increase in cost of sales comes straight out of net profit.

The Really Bright Manufacturing Company Ltd
profit and loss account
for year ended 31st March 2000

	Original £ 000's	Revised £ 000's
Sales	1,200	1,200
Cost of sales	700	850
Gross profit	500	350
Operating expenses	275	275
Net profit	➤225 —————— ➤ 75	
Effect on net profit of stock revaluation		

Amongst the most common reasons for stock value having to be written down, or worse, written off are:

- Goods go past their sell by date and are written down or written off
- Goods become obsolete
- Goods go out of style or fashion
- Goods get damaged
- Goods get miscounted
- Goods get lost
- Goods get stolen.

Gross margin

Just as we use net profit divided by sales to calculate net margin, so we use a similar calculation to work out gross margin.

Formula for gross margin

$$\frac{\text{Gross profit} \times 100}{\text{Sales}} \quad = \quad \%$$

? ## Test Yourself

Using the figures on the following profit and loss account, calculate the effect on gross margin and net margin before and after the stock value adjustment.

**The Really Bright Manufacturing Company Ltd
profit and loss account
for year ended 31st March 2000**

	Original £ 000's	Revised £000's
Sales	1,200	1,200
Cost of sales	700	850
Gross profit	500	350
Operating expenses	275	275
Net profit	225	75

Recall that:

gross margin is: $\quad \dfrac{\text{gross profit} \times 100}{\text{sales}} \quad = \quad \%$

net margin is: $\quad \dfrac{\text{net profit} \times 100}{\text{sales}} \quad = \quad \%$

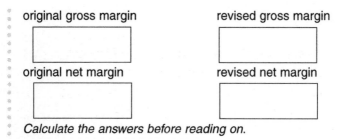

original gross margin

revised gross margin

original net margin

revised net margin

Calculate the answers before reading on.

Answers

Original gross margin: $\dfrac{500 \times 100}{1200}$ = 41.67%

Revised gross margin: $\dfrac{350 \times 100}{1200}$ = 29.17%

Original net margin: $\dfrac{225 \times 100}{1200}$ = 18.75%

Revised net margin: $\dfrac{75 \times 100}{1200}$ = 6.25%

Thus it can be said that any reduction in the value of stock has an impact on gross profit and gross margin and net profit and net margin. As we'll see when we get to other financial measures, the knock-on effect just goes on and on. Think of stock losses as seriously bad news and you won't go far wrong.

NOTE
Some companies may use the term gross profit % and net profit % in place of gross margin and net margin.

Summary

- The profit and loss account is a record of sales, cost of sales, gross profit, operating costs and net profit for a period of time known as an accounting or trading period.
- The profit and loss account is sometimes known as the income or revenue statement.
- The profit and loss account will be headed profit and loss account for period ended 31st March 19__, or some other date.
- From the profit and loss account we can calculate gross and net margin/return on sales and monitor cost of sales and operating costs.

Operating expenses

In addition to cost of sales all companies incur additional operating costs. Salaries, insurance, sales and marketing costs, distribution and many more. Taken together, cost of sales plus operating costs/expenses equal total costs.

For management purposes, operating costs/expenses will be sub-divided into other categories.

Among the most usual are:

- Sales and marketing
- Distribution
- Research and development
- General administration

These headings may be further divided to give more detailed information for more accurate monitoring.

Profit and loss account: Part 2

We know that the bottom line on a profit and loss account is net profit before interest and tax. We also know the reason for it being called the bottom line, this being the point to which most employees will have an influence.

In the profit and loss account shown below you will see that the complete document contains other information.

Farm Rise Ltd
profit and loss account
for period ended 31st March 2000

	Sales	←	TOP LINE
−	Cost of sales		
=	Gross profit		
−	Operating expenses		
=	Net profit before interest and tax	←	BOTTOM LINE
−	Interest		
=	Net profit before tax		
−	Tax		
=	Net Profit After Tax		
−	Dividends		
=	Retained profit for year		
+	Retained profit for previous years		
=	Total accumulated profit		

Now let's add some numbers and see what the finished article looks like.

Farm Rise Ltd
Profit and loss account
For Period Ended 31st March 2000

	£000's		
Sales	100,000		
Cost of sales	60,000		
Gross profit	40,000		
Operating expenses	35,000		
Net profit before interest and tax	5,000	←	BOTTOM LINE
Interest	1,000		
Net profit before tax	4,000		
Tax	1,000		
Net profit after tax	3,000		
Dividends	1,000		
Retained profit for year	2,000		
Retained profit for previous years	25,000		
Total accumulated profit	27,000		

Interest

This is interest charged on loans and is the first cost to be deducted from the bottom line.

Tax

This is Corporation or Profits Tax levied by the Government. Tax rates vary according to company turnover.

Dividends

Think of dividends as being a reward for the shareholders for risking their money in the company.

In the profit and loss account above, we see that the company paid a dividend of £1,000. Had the company decided not to pay a dividend the retained profit for the year would be £3,000 and the total accumulated profit would be £28,000.

There may be times when a company believes that it is in the interest of its shareholders not to pay a dividend in a particular year. It may be planning to purchase another business, invest in fixed assets or embark on a heavy research and development programme. It is usually less expensive to use one's own money than to borrow, where interest will be charged.

In such circumstances the company will be expected to put forward a strong argument to its shareholders. If the shareholders are not convinced they may use their voting power to force the company to reverse the decision.

The 'bottom line' of the Farm Rise profit and loss account is £5,000 but, as can be seen, the final line is total accumulated profit. In a later chapter we shall see that total accumulated profit is the link between the profit and loss account and the balance sheet.

Management and statutory accounts

Before we move on to the Balance Sheet we need to consider **management accounts** and **statutory accounts**:

- What are they?
- What do they include?
- Who uses them?

Management accounts

Most businesses provide managers with financial reports. They're often referred to as the management report or management accounts. These reports are normally intended for internal use only and are usually produced by the finance department or finance controller. They come under a guise of different names:

- Weekly sales report
- Monthly sales review
- Company trading report
- Sales analysis
- Contribution report
- Weekly/monthly profit & loss

Content of management accounts

Just as the name of this financial report will vary from company to company so too will the content. Some companies may choose to use a single sheet of paper with minimum information. Others run to several pages with detailed analysis and commentary.

The decision on the amount of detail, the frequency and who should receive them, varies from one company to another. One company may regard giving too much financial information away as risky. Others work on the basis that too much is better than too little. A supermarket, for instance, may decide to issue a report to its store managers at the close of trading every day. If not, it will almost certainly issue them weekly and monthly.

Just as there are no hard and fast rules regarding content and frequency, neither are their rules for layout and terminology. A common cause of confusion and frustration is often experienced by people who move from one company to another – even between divisions in the same company. Whatever the name, content or frequency of the report, the purpose should be the same: management accounts should help managers to manage more effectively. By comparing actual results with the forecast, managers are able to monitor performance and identify trends.

Statutory accounts

Statutory accounts, as the name suggests, are required by law. Unlike management accounts where there are few rules, statutory accounts have many. The content and format must meet the requirements of various companies Acts, one being that the accounts must be audited by a qualified Chartered Accountant. They are filed and available to public scrutiny at Companies House in Cardiff.

The annual report and accounts of a public listed company often resemble a glossy magazine. They contain articles and photographs of noteworthy achievements throughout the year. Management accounts are used by employees to help make better business decisions. Statutory accounts on the other hand are used by a number of individuals and institutions.

A bank manager will have more than a passing interest in a set of accounts where an overdraft is in place, particularly if the company concerned is a customer of the bank. A City analyst may skip the gloss and glitter and go straight to the balance sheet and profit and loss account. Employees generally head for the section headed 'Directors Remuneration'. Amongst others who use statutory accounts are the Inland Revenue, shareholders and potential shareholders.

Accounting policies

Search through the document and you may find a paragraph outlining the policies under which they have been prepared. For example:

These financial statements have been prepared under the historical cost convention as amended by the revaluation of freehold property in the United Kingdom and in accordance with applicable accounting standards.

Continuing operations include the results of those operations that are to be retained by the Group. Discontinued operations are those businesses whose sale or termination has been completed prior to the period end.

Signed: J. Smith, Auditor

There are four basic principles that apply.

1. *Going concern*
   This simply means that the report has been prepared and the figures reflect the belief and understanding that the business will continue to trade.

2. *Accruals*
   This means that the costs which have been incurred in the period under review have been included regardless of whether they have been paid for.

3. *Consistency*
   This means that the report has been prepared 'consistent with' previous periods. This allows for comparisons to be made.

4. *Prudence*
   This means that the company in general, and the auditors in particular, have adopted a conservative approach. This is not always easy when the Board may wish to include optimistic forecasts to try convince the shareholders that next year really will be better.

The balance sheet

A balance sheet is a summary of assets and liabilities at a particular moment in time. It is often described as a financial snapshot of the business. As with a photograph the subject of course changes before and after the shot is taken. That's just the way it is with assets and liabilities. They change day by day, often hour by hour.

The balance sheet is drawn up at the end of an accounting period and will be headed:

'Balance Sheet as at 31st December 19...'

or any other date that marks the end of the accounting period to which the balance sheet refers.

Simply put, the balance sheet is a summary of the things that an organisation *owns* and *owes* at a particular moment in time.

Assets

Assets are things that the company owns. They can be broadly divided into two categories:

1. Current assets
2. Fixed assets.

Current assets comprise:

- stock
- debtors
- cash

Current assets are known as the working assets of the business. They need to be working and turning over as fast as possible. The faster a company is able to turn its stock into debtors or cash, and then use the cash to operate the business on a day-to-day basis, the more profitable it will become.

Fixed assets comprise:

- land
- buildings
- machinery etc.

These tend to move more slowly. Fixed assets are often funded from long-term loans. They are assets which the business may need in order to operate, such as a building, or computers or vehicles to deliver goods. Whereas current assets may be described as short-term assets, fixed assets may be described as long-term assets.

Current assets

Stock

Stock may also be described as inventory. As we saw earlier when we examined cost of sales, stock may be found in three forms:

- raw materials
- work-in-progress (or work-in-process)
- finished goods.

On the balance sheet, stock is valued at cost or the amount which it is expected to 'realise'. It should not be too difficult to think of reasons why a company may decide to re-value stock: market conditions change; slow moving stock may remain in the warehouse or on the shelf unless reduced in price; a company may need to make room for a new product, or simply require cash. There are many reasons why stock may be re-valued.

Keeping stock 'on the books' at an artificially high price is not good management practice. It is not prudent and is against the fundamental accounting principle mentioned earlier: *prudence*.

Debtors

Debtors are people to whom goods or services have been supplied but for which payment has not yet been received. In some countries you may find the term 'Accounts Receivable' used in place of debtors. Similarly, the term 'Accounts Payable' may be used in place of creditors. Creditors, as we shall see shortly, are people to whom we, the company, owe money.

In an ideal world all companies would prefer to have their goods or services exchanged for cash. It reduces risk and improves cashflow. But not every business is able to get paid immediately. There are times when customers expect credit. When a company delivers goods or services and raises an invoice for future payment, the transaction is listed under debtors. Strange as it may seem when a company gives credit to a customer that customer becomes a debtor – another reason why non-financial managers sometimes struggle with the language.

The amount shown on the balance sheet under debtors is the amount of credit the company has allowed and expects to be fully repaid within twelve months of the date of the balance sheet.

Cash
Cash is the lifeblood of business. It is used to pay wages and salaries, suppliers, rent, tax – in fact all costs.

Good cash management is an essential element of financial survival. It is not to be confused with profit. Indeed, the vast majority of companies who go bankrupt do so making a profit. More often than not they simply run out of cash. See the later section on cashflow.

Fixed assets

An organisation cannot own assets of any kind without first having the money to buy them. We shall consider the different sources of funding shortly.

Together, current and fixed assets are known as total assets.

By knowing how much money a company has invested in total assets and using the net profit figure from the profit and loss account we are able to calculate return on investment.

Return on investment (ROI)

Return on Investment is a key financial performance measure. It shows the return a company is getting on its investment in total assets. It is not possible to calculate ROI from the profit and loss account or balance sheet individually. Both documents are required. The net profit will be found on the profit and loss account and total assets on the balance sheet.

NOTE

Whenever you see a ratio with the word 'return' in the title it refers to net profit before interest and tax, otherwise known as operating profit.

Formula for return on investment:

$$\frac{\text{Net profit} \times 100}{\text{Total assets}} \quad = \quad \%$$

Think of net profit as the *result* or *return* and total assets as the *investment* or *resource*.

$$\frac{\textit{Net profit}}{\text{Total assets}} \quad = \quad \frac{\textit{Result}}{\text{Resource}} \quad = \quad \frac{\textit{Return}}{\text{Investment}}$$

To improve return on investment a company aims to maximise the return and minimise the investment parts of the equation.

Before we move on and see how useful the ROI formula can be we need to consider alternative names by which return on investment may also be known.

Recall that net profit has alternative names:

- operating profit
- trading profit
- net profit before tax
- pre-tax profit
- earnings
- bottom line

It should come as no surprise then to discover that return on investment may also have a different name and abbreviation. In place of return on investment, be prepared to see:

- return on assets or ROA
- return on total assets or ROTA
- return on assets managed or ROAM
- return on managed assets or ROMA

Example

A company has a net profit of £10,500 and total assets of £140,000. The return on investment is therefore:

$$\frac{\text{net profit}}{\text{total assets}} \quad \frac{£10,500}{£140,000} \times 100 = 7.5\%$$

? Test Yourself

Calculate the return on investment for the following companies:

	Company A1 (£million)	Company B1 (£million)	Company C1 (£million)
Net profit	4.2	3.4	5.1
Total assets	30.8	25.4	34.5

	Company A1	Company B1	Company C1
Return on investment			

The correct answers are on the following page

ANSWERS

	Company A1	Company B1	Company C1
Return on investment	13.64%	13.38%	14.79%

A question frequently asked is: 'Is there a percentage regarded as acceptable or good?' Unfortunately, no. A company should aim to get the highest return on its investment in total assets, consistent with providing its customers with quality products and quality service.

To be simplistic one might take the rate of return offered by a building society or bank. To close a business down and re-invest the money in that way would be a little drastic. A company, and indeed shareholders will want to know how efficiently the business is being managed. The ROI formula will reveal that.

Whereas return on sales focuses on sales, costs and margins, return on investment focuses on company assets.

The ROI formula may be used to make comparisons between similar sized companies in the same industry. It may also be used to compare one division of a company with another, or one region with another. A company may need to choose between making an investment in one location or another. While factors such as availability of labour, distribution costs and grants or subsidies will be taken into account, the final decision is likely to be influenced by the projected return on investment.

Return on capital employed (ROCE), otherwise known as Return on net assets (RONA)

While the calculation is different from ROI the principle remains the same. The aim is to maximise the top half of the equation, the net profit, and minimise the bottom half, which is capital employed or net assets. Companies may choose to use one or the other or both. One being return on total assets and the other return on net assets.

Before we look at capital employed or net assets it will help to become more familiar with the balance sheet.

You probably have a hobby or interest outside work. It may be football, cricket, tennis, fishing, or another sporting activity. It may be that you have an interest in horses or dogs. Think for a moment about your favourite hobby or interest. For the purpose of what we are about to create together the actual hobby is of secondary importance. It's your opportunity to personalise the next section of the book.

Imagine that you have identified a gap in the market place for a specialist magazine in the area which just happens to be your hobby. Think of a title for your magazine. Together we will build a company around your idea for the magazine.

Step 1
You have carried out extensive market research to back up your hunch and produced a business plan that you take along to the bank. The bank like what they see and you

form a company using the title of the magazine as the company name.

Your company will be called 'The .... Magazine Company Ltd'

You plan to buy the raw materials to produce the magazine, write and edit it with your own staff. You plan to sell it through retail outlets. You have £5000 to invest. You decide to invite like-minded people with a similar interest to invest in the business. You find five willing participants and they each invest £2,000. You have £10,000 from outside investors and £5,000 of your own making an 'initial share capital' of £15,000.

In the pages that follow you will see how a balance sheet fits together and how it can be used to monitor:

- working capital
- return on net assets
- return on capital employed
- current ratio
- quick ratio
- stock turn
- debtor days
- creditor days

We will use a side by side balance sheet known as dual aspect. It's no longer used in management accounts or statutory accounts but is used for educational and training purposes. We will transfer the information to the more familiar vertical format version at the end of the section. You will see how the vertical format lends itself to year on year comparisons.

Now, let's get The .... Magazine Company Ltd off the ground.

At the moment all you have is £15,000 and a lot of self-belief and enthusiasm. In order to produce the magazine what will you need? Answer: assets.

You will need some fixed assets such as a printing machine and a place to operate it from: a building or premises of some sort. You will need fixtures and fittings for the office. You will need a computer, desks and chairs and perhaps a small van for deliveries.

A company cannot have assets without first having the funds to acquire them. The only funding available at the moment is the £15,000 of share capital otherwise known as shareholders' funds. Clearly, £15,000 will not go very far.

When a business is formed money can come from two sources: the shareholders or from borrowed money. When the business is in a position to be able to generate profit it will have another source of funding: retained profit. In the beginning it must rely entirely on shareholders and/or borrowings.

To fund the building, printing machine and van you decide to take a long-term loan. This is known as a long-term liability. Because you expect the business to flourish and survive you decide that a long-term loan should be used to fund some of the fixed or long-term assets. Having moved into your premises and installed the printing machine, you will begin to print and sell the magazine. In doing so you will create your own current assets comprising stock, debtors and cash.

The following diagram is a dual aspect version of the balance sheet for The ....Magazine Company Ltd. The left hand side tells us where the money or funding has come from, and the right hand side where the money has gone to. That is why a balance sheet will always balance. It is not called balance sheet for that reason however. Originally it was a list of balances and that is how the name came into being.

The .... Magazine Company Ltd
Extract from balance sheet
for the period ended 31st December 2000

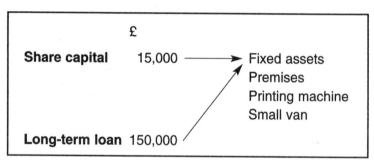

As the business begins to produce the magazine it will need to purchase raw materials such as paper and ink. Now, remembering that the only source of funding available is either from shareholders or borrowings, you have a choice. It's unlikely that you would approach the shareholders to provide more share capital to help the business purchase raw materials. Should all else fail, that might be your only option, but highly unlikely and not to be recommended. Taking a long-term loan to fund the purchase of raw materials is also out of the question.

Think about it for a moment. Where else might the business

obtain funding for the raw materials that are absolutely essential to produce the magazine? There are two choices: one is less expensive than the other.

The first choice would be to find a supplier of paper and ink and obtain supplies from them. You might be able to negotiate credit terms and pay 30 days from receipt of goods. A monthly account from most suppliers is quite usual. As the business becomes established it may be possible to negotiate longer periods of credit. This will be helpful for cashflow, as we will see shortly. Initially suppliers will want to proceed with caution and are likely to want to apply an upper credit limit. This will limit their own exposure to risk.

Should this not be enough to meet demand, the other source of short-term funding is the bank. Since they were impressed with your market research and business plan they may grant an overdraft facility to the company. It should be remembered that an overdraft carries with it certain obligations for the directors of the company and of course interest charges. Wherever possible the company would be better advised to use suppliers' credit than borrow from the bank. One source of funding is free of interest and the other attracts it.

Whether the funding is obtained from suppliers or from the bank they will be listed on the balance sheet under the heading creditors. They are both short-term loans. A loan is called short-term when it is expected to be repaid within twelve months. Anything over twelve months is a long-term loan.

Having obtained short-term funding from suppliers and the

bank, the company converts raw materials into work-in-progress and finally into finished goods. The magazine proves a hit with the customers and from a modest beginning sales gradually increase until the sales forecast in the business plan is exceeded. Let's see how the Balance Sheet looks with the new information added.

**The .... Magazine Company Ltd
balance sheet for the period ended 31st December 2000**

	£		£
Share capital	15,000 →	**Fixed assets**	165,000
	↑	Premises	
		Printing machine	
		Small van	
Long-term loan	150,000		
Current liabilities		**Current assets**	
Short-term loan	5,000	Stock	7,000
Trade Creditors	8,000	Debtors	18,000
		Cash	1,000

Long-term loans are classified as long-term liabilities.

Long-term liabilities plus current liabilities are called total liabilities.

At the end of the year the profit and loss account shows retained profit of £13,000. As the company has only been trading for 12 months there are no profits from previous years so it is the retained profit of £13,000 that will be transferred to the balance sheet. On its journey it will undergo a name change: from retained profit to reserves.

When reserves are added to the initial investment of the shareholders (share capital) the combined total is known as owners' equity or shareholders' funds. You saw earlier that fixed assets plus current assets equals total assets.

So, owners' equity or shareholders' funds plus total liabilities equals total assets.

Let's complete the picture and check to see if our balance sheet balances.

The ………….. Magazine Company Ltd
balance sheet for the period ended 31st December 2000

	£			
Share capital	15,000	) OWNERS'	**Fixed assets**	165,000
Reserves	13,000	) EQUITY	Premises	
			Printing machine	
			Small van	
Long-term loan	150,000	)		
		) TOTAL		
Current liabilities		) LIABILITIES	**Current assets**	
Short-term loan	5,000	)	Stock	7,000
Trade Creditors	8,000	)	Debtors	18,000
			Cash	1,000
OWNERS' EQUITY + TOTAL LIABILITIES	191,000	=	TOTAL ASSETS	191,000

At the beginning of this section we explained that the balance sheet is more commonly produced in a vertical format so that year-on-year comparisons may be made. In the next diagram you will see a Balance Sheet for The Quick Dry Paint Company Ltd. The company has been trading for a number of years and so, as one might expect, has accumulated profit over the years it's been trading. Each year retained profit from that year is added to retained profit from all previous years to give total accumulated profit. This is the link between the profit and loss account and the balance sheet. It is the total accumulated profit shown on the profit and loss account which is transferred to the balance sheet. On the balance sheet, total accumulated profit may be described as reserves.

The Quick Dry Paint Company
Balance Sheet as at 31st December 1998

MONEY FROM HERE		IS INVESTED HERE	
	£000's		£000's
Owners' equity		**Fixed assets**	
Share Capital	100	Buildings	100
Accumulated profit	50	Plant and Equipment	100
Long-term loan	195		
Current liabilities		**Current assets**	
Short-terms loans	60	Stock	80
Trade creditors	95	Debtors	120
		Cash	100
Owners' equity + Total liabilities	500 =	**Total assets**	500

NOTE

- A balance sheet always balances
- In this example the left hand side provides the funds for the right hand side

- Long-term funding is generally used for long-term or slow moving assets
- Short-term funding is generally used for short-term or fast moving assets.

In the following example you will see the same balance sheet in the more traditional vertical format.

The Quick Dry Paint Company
balance sheet as at 31st December 1998

	£000's	
Fixed assets		
Buildings	100	
Plant and Equipment	100	
Current assets		TOTAL ASSETS
Stock	80	
Debtors	120	
Cash	100	
Creditors		
Long-term loan	195	
Current liabilities		TOTAL LIABILITIES
Short-term loans	60	
Trade creditors	95	

Net Current Assets (Current assets less Current liabilities)

Net Assets (Total Assets less Total Liabilities)

FINANCED BY:

Original/share capital	100
Accumulated profit	50

Note the new terms on the above Balance Sheet.

Net assets (sometimes called capital employed) is total assets less total liabilities.

Net assets **always** equal shareholders' funds (sometimes called owners' equity).

Net current assets (sometimes called working capital) are current assets less current liabilities.

More business ratios

Return on net assets (sometimes known as return on capital employed)

Return on net assets, also known as return on capital employed, requires information from both the profit and loss account and the balance sheet. The 'return' as always is net profit from the profit and loss account.

Net assets or capital employed is sometimes shown as a separate line on the balance sheet. If not, to work it out all you need to do is deduct total liabilities from total assets.

Net current assets (otherwise known as working capital)

To calculate a company's net current assets or working capital you need to take the current asset figure from the balance sheet and deduct current liabilities.

The following extract from the balance sheet of The Quick Dry Paint Company shows:

	Year 1 £'000	Year 2 £'000
Current assets:		
Stock	80	140
Debtors	120	160
Cash	100	100
	300	400

Current liabilities:		
Short-term loan	60	60
Trade creditors	95	105
	155	165

In Year 1, working capital is £145, (**CA** £300 less **CL** £155)

In Year 2, working capital is £235 (**CA** £400 less **CL** £165)

Working capital has increased and the main reason appears to be that the company is carrying more stock and has more debtors. There may of course be perfectly valid reasons for these increases. The company may have added a new product to the range, or be in the middle of a sales drive where credit was offered as an incentive to customers to buy. Whenever you see an increase in working capital ask questions to establish the reason for the change. If it's acceptable don't concern yourself. If it's not acceptable … get concerned! Find out why it's happened and take steps to bring it in line with the workable minimum.

Current ratio

Current assets divided by current liabilities. A company is said to have a healthy current ratio when the ratio is 2:1. The rationale being that should the company be called upon to meet its short-term obligations (current liabilities) but has the capability to cover that by a factor of 2 from the amount it has invested in current assets – that's a healthy position to be in.

Quick ratio

Quick ratio is sometimes known as the acid test. It is similar in many respects to current ratio with one notable exception – we remove 'stock' from the equation. The formula for quick ratio is:

Current assets less stock divided by current liabilities

Imagine a situation where a company has a current ratio of 2:1 and then asks the bank manager for a larger overdraft. On such occasions the bank manager may want to apply the acid test before making a decision.

Why you may well ask, should that be necessary. What does the acid test reveal that current ratio doesn't? Think about it for a moment. Current assets less stock leaves debtors and cash. By eliminating stock from the equation the bank remove the one area that might cause difficulty should anything go wrong and they're left to pick up the pieces. Stock may include obsolete lines or damaged goods which may have to be written down or written off.

The quick ratio is current ratio with the main element of risk removed.

Stock turn

The formula is sales divided by cost of sales. It shows the number of times a company is turning over its stock in the period under review. There is no rule of thumb other than to say that a company should aim to get the highest stock turn possible. By turning stock into debtors, and debtors into cash in the shortest possible time, the company will generate cash to run the business. Fast stock turn is one of the ingredients in the recipe for financial success.

When considering stock turn avoid the trap of making

comparisons between one industry and another. One company selling expensive antiques may be quite happy to have a stock turn of four times a year. If the local fishmonger had the same stock turn he would soon be out of business. By all means make comparisons between one company and another in the same industry. A furniture retailer might like to compare stock turn with other furniture retailers. That's OK and could be helpful, but to compare a furniture retailer with, say, a jewelry retailer will be misleading.

Debtor days

The formula for debtor days is:

$$\frac{\text{Debtors} \times 365}{\text{Sales}}$$

The ratio is an indication of the number of days debtors are outstanding. Let's say that you want to calculate debtor days for a particular company. You will need to go to the balance sheet to find the debtors figure and the profit and loss account for sales.

Example:

$$\frac{\text{Debtors}}{\text{Sales}} \quad \frac{£25,000 \times 365}{£130,000} = 70 \text{ days}$$

If the company's trading terms were 30 days this would indicate that things were not as they ought to be. In this case you would investigate further. Most companies will have a debtors list showing the age of the debt. The list will normally be broken down into 30 days, 60 days, 90 days and beyond. An increase in debtor days may be an indication of a quality problem or a slack credit control policy. You may also want to know how many customers the debtors figure represents. Is it one customer who owes £25,000 or 25 customers each owing £1,000?

One of the secrets of financial success is a healthy cashflow. That is achieved when stock is turned into cash and debtors, and then debtors into cash as quickly as possible.

Creditor days

The formula for creditor days is:

$$\frac{\text{Creditors} \times 365}{\text{Cost of Sales}}$$

The ratio is an indication of how quickly the company is paying its creditors. Just as with debtor days you will need to go to the balance sheet and the profit and loss account to obtain the figures. Cost of sales is on the profit and loss account and creditors is on the balance sheet.

We've suggested earlier that it makes sense to fund purchases by taking advantage of credit terms offered by suppliers, rather than paying interest on a bank overdraft. However, companies with a reputation for late payment often find themselves on a supplier's stop list.

Remember that your creditor days are somebody else's debtor days.

More business ratios

Gross margin

$$\frac{\text{Gross Profit} \times 100}{\text{Sales}} \qquad \frac{8,000}{20,000} \qquad = \qquad 40\%$$

Net margin (return on sales)

$$\frac{\text{Net profit} \times 100}{\text{Sales}} \qquad \frac{2,000 \times 100}{20,000} \qquad = \qquad 10\%$$

Return on investment

$$\frac{\text{Net profit} \times 100}{\text{Total assets}} \qquad \frac{2,000}{10,000} \qquad = \qquad 20\%$$

Return on net assets (capital employed)

$$\frac{\text{Net profit} \times 100}{\text{Total assets} - \text{total liabilities}} \qquad \frac{2,000}{6,000 - 4,000} \qquad = \qquad 33.33\%$$

Current ratio

$$\frac{\text{current assets}}{\text{current liabilities}} \qquad \frac{6,000}{3,000} \qquad = \qquad 2\text{:}1$$

Quick ratio

$$\frac{\text{current assets} - \text{stock}}{\text{current liabilities}} \qquad \frac{6,000 - 3,000}{3,000} \qquad = \qquad 1\text{:}1$$

Stock turn (short-cut method)

$$\frac{\text{Sales}}{\text{Stock}} \qquad \frac{20,000}{3,000} \qquad = \qquad 6.6 \text{ times}$$

Stock turn (correct method)

$$\frac{\text{Cost of sales}}{\text{Stock}} \qquad \frac{12,000}{3,000} \qquad = \qquad 4 \text{ times}$$

Debtor days

$$\frac{\text{Debtors} \times 365}{\text{Sales}} \qquad \frac{2,000 \times 365}{20,000} \qquad = \qquad 36 \text{ days}$$

Creditor days

$$\frac{\text{Creditors} \times 365}{\text{Cost of sales}} \qquad \frac{1,500 \times 365}{12,000} \qquad = \qquad 45 \text{ days}$$

Budgets and cashflow

Ask almost any employee if they have anything to do with the preparation of the company cashflow statement and the majority will say no. Ask the same employees if they have anything to do with the preparation of the company budget and some will say yes.

The fact is that every employee has something to do with both.

A manager may be asked to predict how much his or her department will require by way of funding in the next financial year. Common practice is to use last year's budget as the starting point although some companies prefer to use what's known as zero-based budgeting. This ignores what happened before and builds the picture from scratch – hence zero-based.

The budget is an expression of future plans in financial terms. The budget is a form of control and most organisations use the budget as the benchmark against which weekly and monthly performance is measured. In one column you may see 'budgeted' sales. Next to that a column headed 'actual' sales and finally a column headed 'variance.'

A budget will typically cover a full twelve months trading period but in the following example we will look at the first period only. In most organisations once the budget has been set and signed off, nobody is allowed to make changes. The budget becomes a sacrosanct document. This is why so much effort is put into the preparation of the budget to make sure it is as accurate as possible.

They say that the only thing constant in life is change. In most companies the only thing that will not change is the budget. Obviously between the preparation of the budget and the time it is used things always change. It is impossible to foresee all of the things that will take place in the future. All we can do is use our knowledge and previous experiences and add to that our expectations of future events. Events may have an internal or external influence. Some will be within our control, others outside our control.

Some companies rely on the weather for their business. We all know how unpredictable that can be. If you've ever planned a barbecue in a British summer you will know the problem. If your business depends on the sun shining at a particular time to achieve budgeted sales you will appreciate that all the skill and experience in the world is not enough to guarantee what the weather will be like on the day.

A company might build sales of a new product into the budget. That product might hit technical problems that cause the launch to be delayed. There would be little point in continuing throughout the rest of the year, comparing 'actual' against 'budget' although some companies may insist on it. It is more likely that the company will take the view that it should review the situation and produce a revised budget or revised forecast, and work to that.

The company may still wish to compare actual performance with the original budget but, having taken the new factors into consideration, a new column will typically be added headed 'Revised Budget' or 'Revised Forecast'. The last column may be headed 'Year to Date' or 'Cumulative' and is used to show the cumulative position for actual sales.

Budget for period ending 2000

	January					**February**				
	Budget	Revised Forecast	Actual	Variance	YTD	Budget	Revised Forecast	Actual	Variance	YTD
Sales	100	80	82	+2	+2	120	110	105	−5	−3

The budget will not only include predictions in terms of sales and costs but also take account of changes in sales strategy, products, services and staffing levels. Performance against budget or revised forecast will usually be found in the weekly or monthly set of management accounts, and distributed to the appropriate department: Research and Development, Human Resources, Sales and Marketing, Warehouse and Distribution and any other department where performance is measured.

Cashflow

A company needs to convert the budget or revised forecast into a statement of cash flowing into and out of the business. At the beginning of this section we said:

'Ask almost any employee if they have anything to do with the preparation of the company cashflow statement and the majority will say no.

Ask the same employees if they have anything to do with the preparation of the company budget, and some will say yes'.

Since every employee's costs are included in the budget,

every employee influences it. Each Head of Department will be asked for their input and when everything is added together the company has an overall plan which becomes the budget.

The cashflow statement is the interpretation of the budget in terms of cash flowing into the business and cash flowing out. Therefore everybody who has an input into a departmental budget has an influence on cashflow. If a junior secretary needs a new computer, salesperson a new vehicle or factory manager new machinery, at some point cash will be needed to fund them. The cashflow statement is a prediction and for accuracy must include all such requirements. Leaving things out of the prediction may lead to the statement: *'Sorry, you can't have it. It's not in the budget.'*

Just as a household has income and expenditure throughout the year so too do companies. On the next two pages you will see how a cashflow statement may be used to help a family run their finances and then a typical cashflow statement used by companies.

Household budget for year ending 31st December 2000

£'s

	Jan	Feb	March	April	May	June	July	Aug	Sep	Oct	Nov	Dec	TOTAL
RECEIPTS													
Salary	1,000	1,000	1,000	1,000	1,000	1,000	1,000	1,000	1,000	1,000	1,000	1,000	12,000
Bonus							1,000						1,000
Partner	650	650	650	650	650	650	650	650	650	650	650	650	7,800
Bonus												350	350
Total receipts	1,650	1,650	1,650	1,650	1,650	1,650	2,650	1,650	1,650	1,650	1,650	2,000	21,150
PAYMENTS													
Mortgage	750	750	750	750	750	750	750	750	750	750	750	750	9,000
Life Insurance	25	25	25	25	25	25	25	25	25	25	25	25	300
Council tax	100	100	100	100	100	100	100	100	100	100	100	100	1,200
Pension	100	100	100	100	100	100	100	100	100	100	100	100	1,200
Electricity	0	0	200	0	0	200	0	0	250	0	0	200	850
Health Insurance	50	50	50	50	50	50	50	50	50	50	50	50	600
TV License	0	0	0	110	0	0	0	0	0	0	0	0	110
Satellite TV	15	15	15	125	15	15	15	15	15	15	15	15	180
Car	200	200	200	200	200	200	200	200	200	200	200	200	2,400
Car tax				155									155
Holiday								2000					2000
Miscellaneous	400	400	400	400	400	400	400	400	400	400	400	400	4800
Total payments	1,640	1,640	1,840	1,905	1,640	1,840	1,640	3,640	1,890	1,640	1,640	1,840	22,795
Net cashflow	10	10	-190	-255	10	10	1,010	-1,990	-240	10	10	160	-1,645
Opening balance	500	510	560	370	115	125	135	1,345	-645	-885	-875	-865	-705
Closing balance	510	560	370	115	125	135	1345	-645	-885	-875	-865	-705	-2350

NOTE: The closing balance for December 1999 is carried forward to become the opening balance for January 2000

Cashflow forecast for year ending 31st December 2000

£'s

	Jan	Feb	March	April	May	June	July	Aug	Sep	Oct	Nov	Dec	TOTAL
RECEIPTS													
Debtors	80,000	45,000	60,000	50,000	50,000	60,000	60,000	55,000	90,000	90,000	90,000	90,000	820,000
Cash sales	60,000	50,000	50,000	50,000	50,000	55,000	55,000	50,000	55,000	60,000	65,000	70,000	670,000
Sale of fixed assets					20,000								20,000
Total receipts	140,000	95,000	110,000	100,000	120,000	115,000	115,000	105,000	145,000	150,000	155,000	160,000	1,510,000
PAYMENTS													
Creditors	90,000	90,000	80,000	75,000	60,000	50,000	50,000	50,000	75,000	75,000	75,000	75,000	845,000
Rent	4,000	4,000	4,000	4,000	4,000	4,000	6,000	6,000	6,000	6,000	6,000	6,000	60,000
Salaries (net)	8,000	8,000	8,000	8,000	8,000	8,000	16,000	16,000	16,000	16,000	16,000	16,000	144,000
Pensions	1,000	1,000	1,000	1,000	1,000	1,000	2,000	2,000	2,000	2,000	2,000	2,000	18,000
Insurance	1,000	1,000	1,000	1,000	1,000	1,000	1500	1500	1500	1500	1500	1500	15,000
Fixed assets							80,000	75,000					155,000
VAT		35,0000			37,000			28,000		45,000			145,000
Vehicles	3,000	3,000	3,000	3,000	3,000	3,000	3,000	3,000	3,000	3,000	3,000	3,000	36,000
Total payments	107,000	142,000	97,000	92,000	114,000	67,000	158,500	181,500	118,500	103,500	148,500	103,500	1,433,000
Net cashflow	33,000	-47,000	13,000	8,000	6,000	48,000	-43,500	-76,500	26,500	46,500	6,500	56,500	77,000
Opening balance	2,000	35,000	-12,000	1,000	9,000	15,000	63,000	19,500	-57,000	-30,500	16,000	22,500	79,000
Closing balance	35,000	-12,000	1,000	9,000	15,000	63,000	19,500	-57,000	-30,500	16,000	22,500	79,000	156,000

Break-even analysis
Fixed and variable costs

All businesses incur costs to operate. These costs, also called expenses, can be broadly divided into two categories:

- fixed
- variable.

Different businesses may use different criteria to categorise their costs but the most widely accepted definitions are:

Fixed costs: *do not* vary in line with output. In other words they stay constant regardless of the amount of goods the business produces or sells. Executive salaries, rent, rates, leasing payments, interest on loans, insurance etc need to be paid month in month out, irrespective of sales or production. These are all examples of fixed costs.

Variables cost: *do* vary in line with output. In other words they increase/decrease in relation to production or sales. The more goods the company produces the more raw materials it requires and so raw materials would be regarded as a variable cost.

Most factories include energy, gas, water, and electricity as a cost directly related to output and therefore classify them as a variable cost. Overtime and sales commission are also variable costs.

In some organisations variable costs may be seen as those costs that are directly related to the main activity of the business and consist of direct labour and direct materials, which is an alternative name for raw materials. Some organisations use a combination of both definitions to categorise their variable costs. The golden rule is 'be consistent'.

Note

Fixed costs plus variable costs equals total costs

Information on fixed and variable costs enables us to calculate contribution. Contribution is the amount of money left over from sales after deducting variable costs.

The formula for contribution is:

Sales less variable cost equals contribution

Let's imagine a situation where you've been invited to help raise funds for the local children's playgroup. You've been asked to calculate the number of tickets that need to be sold in order to make a profit. To do so you decide to create a break-even chart to determine the point at which the event will produce sufficient income to cover both fixed and variable costs.

Background
The Playgroup committee decide to hold a film show in the village hall and invite parents and their children to come along to see a short film on cats and dogs and other domestic pets. Your task is to advise the committee on the viability of the project.

The committee plan to hire a hall, rent a video, advertise the event and print and sell tickets. All of these will be fixed costs. In other words these costs must be paid for whether or not anybody turns up. Fixed costs come to £40.00. One of the committee members offers to provide tea and soft drinks for everybody who attends. You agree to cover their cost of £1.00 per person. Tea and soft drinks will be variable costs.

You decide to sell tickets at £2.00 each out of which you will pay £1.00 for the tea and soft drinks. You now have all the information to build the break-even chart. Remember:

Sales (£2.00) less variable costs (£1.00) equals contribution £1.00 towards fixed and variable costs and thereafter profit.

Step 1
The vertical axis will show the income and the horizontal axis the number of tickets sold. First we draw a line to represent the fixed costs of £40.00.

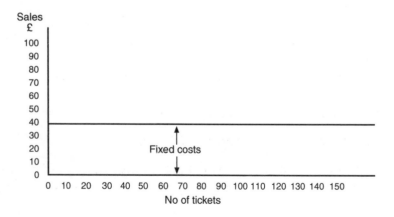

Step 2
The next step is draw a line on top of the fixed costs to represent variable costs of £1.00 per ticket.

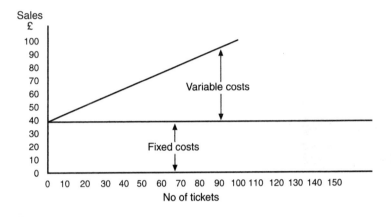

Step 3
Here we add another line to represent sales at £2.00 per ticket. You will see that when you have sold 20 tickets at £2.00 you have enough income to pay for your fixed costs.

Variable costs come on top of fixed costs.

Break-even is the point where the sales line intersects with total costs. This is the point at which you begin to make a profit.

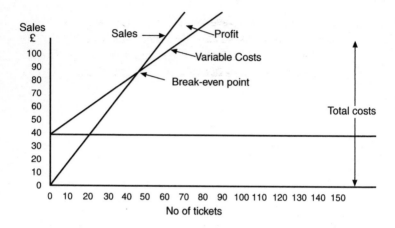

For most managers, costs that come directly under their control are 'controllable' and are by definition 'variable'. In most situations variable costs will be easier to reduce than fixed costs. Reducing variable costs increases contribution to fixed costs and profit and the break-even point will be lower too.

? Test Yourself

Q1. If the sales price is raised to £2.50 how many tickets need to be sold to cover fixed costs?

Q2. If variable costs are reduced to £0.50 and the sales price remains at £2.00 how many tickets need to be sold before the event begins to make a profit?

Answers

Q1. If the sales price were increased to £2.50 per ticket

you need to sell 16 tickets to cover fixed costs of £40.00.

Q2. If the variable costs were reduced to £0.50 and the sales price was kept at £2.00, contribution would increase to £1.50. Under this scenario you will need to sell 27 tickets to cover the fixed costs of £40.00.

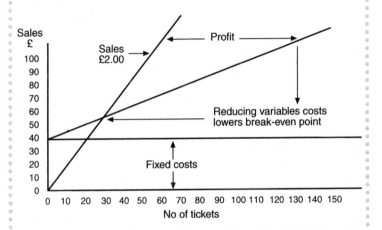

The productivity equation

So far in measuring financial performance we have used ratios. All ratios in this book are based on the productivity equation of output over input, where output is the result and input the resource. By multiplying the answer by 100 the bottom half of the equation is then expressed as a percentage of the top half.

Example
Return on investment:

$$\frac{\text{Net profit}}{\text{Total assets}} \quad \frac{£500}{£6000} \quad \times 100 = 8.33\%$$

You will remember too that to improve return on investment you need to maximise the output and minimise the input.

? **Test Yourself**

Q1. What does an organisation need to do in order to maximise net profit?

Q2. What does an organisation need to do to minimise investment in total assets?

Q3 We said that net profit is also known as the bottom line. Why is this when interest, tax, dividends and retained profit all fall below net profit on the profit and loss account?

Answers
Q1. Any improvement in sales and/or reduction in cost of sales will improve gross profit. Any reduction in

operating costs will increase net profit. You should have said each of these actions or any combination of them will maximise net profit.

Q2. To minimise investment in total assets one would first look at current assets because it is often easier to reduce stock, debtors and cash than it is to reduce fixed assets which tend to take longer.

Q3. In most organisations, managers and employees have a direct influence over sales, cost of sales and operating expenses. Since sales less cost of sales equals gross profit, and gross profit less operating costs equals net profit, that's as far as their influence goes, hence the bottom line.

Productivity

It's almost impossible to pick up a newspaper, listen to the news on the radio or watch the daily round-up of business news items on television without the word 'productivity' being mentioned.

Productivity is often used to illustrate differences in manufacturing performance between one company and another, and one industry and another. You may hear that a certain car manufacturer claims to have higher productivity than its competitors, or that one of its plants is more productive than another. This may be used as the reason for moving production from one site to another.

Car manufacturers may describe productivity as the number of vehicles produced per employee, per day, per week, per month, per year etc. By and large improvements in productivity will lead to improvements in profitability.

Let's consider a few more productivity measures. In each case you will see that even with no change in input any improvement in output will lead to an improvement in results. The productivity equation can be used by everybody in every organisation to improve company results. Let's say that a retail company wishes to improve it's sales per square metre. The first step would be to produce a benchmark by keeping track of the sales per square metre over a period of time. By monitoring sales per hour or sales per day the retailer will identify patterns or trends in trading activity.

Some years ago the author was involved in a retail study. Thirty ladies fashion retail stores in the UK took part in the exercise. The company was about to introduce a new sales training programme and the Managing Director insisted on having measures in place that would highlight the effect of the training. The productivity equation was employed to measure a 'before and after' situation in the following areas:

1. Sales per employee
2. Sales per square foot
3. Sales per hour
4. Sales per day
5. Changing room sales
6. Sales per department
7. Average transaction value
8. Multiple sales

The results needed to be statistically valid so for a period of three months prior to the training taking place each store manager was asked to keep records under these eight headings where it was hoped that training would have an impact. Thirty stores took part in the trial. They were divided into 15 matched pairs. Each pair of stores was managed by the same regional manager and produced very similar results week by week.

At the end of the pre-training trial period the company had all the evidence it needed to be able to make comparisons in performance between the 15 pairs of stores.

The next step was to train the sales staff at half the stores and use the other half as the control group. The results of the survey proved very revealing and the training was quickly extended to the other stores in the group.

Warwick University designed the trial and drew attention to the dangers of the *Pareto effect*, i.e. if the control group discovered that they were being used as the benchmark to see how much more the trained group could sell, they might just be motivated to try harder and destroy the validity of the trial. To overcome this no mention of training was made until the last minute. Managers were then sworn to secrecy, but company grapevines being what they are, it was decided to monitor all results for a period of three months after the training took place. This would be long enough to negate the Pareto effect.

One of the more interesting facts to emerge from the trial came from using the productivity equation to measure the number of transactions per hour divided by the number of customer opportunities (customers entering the store). The sharp rise in productivity was evident not only in the newly trained group but also in the stores used as the control group. Productivity increased dramatically between the hours of 3.00pm and 5.30pm on Saturdays. Further investigation revealed that customers had a tendency to shop around during the day and then, having decided which item they preferred, returned to that store to make a purchase. At a time of the day when shop assistants were beginning to wind down and thinking about what they would be wearing that evening, customers were becoming easier to sell to.

If the same productivity measure had been applied to the competition it's most probable that they too were having these same sales opportunities.

? ## Test Yourself

Think about the key performance indicators in your company. Think how you might use the productivity equation to monitor results. You might be surprised at what's there right under your nose.

The final test

At the beginning of the book you were invited to complete a self assessment test to establish your financial knowledge of the information contained in this book. Now is your chance to see how much more financial know-how you have gained.

If you found the questions a little daunting at the beginning we hope that as a result of completing the book and the exercise, you will have gained more knowledge and more confidence to deal with basic financial issues.

GOOD LUCK.

? **Test Yourself**

FINAL TEST

Self Assessment – Financial Awareness

Please indicate whether the following statements are true or false.

	T	F
1. The top line of the profit and loss account shows the owners' equity	☐	☐
2. Working capital is the same as net assets.	☐	☐
3. The balance sheet is sometimes referred to as a financial snapshot of a business.	☐	☐
4. The assets of a business are funded by debtors	☐	☐
5. Cost of sales is equal to opening stock plus purchases less closing stock.	☐	☐

	T	F
6. Gross margin is usually expressed as gross profit divided by sales multiplied by 100.	☐	☐
7. A current ratio of 1:1 is considered healthy.	☐	☐
8. Current liabilities usually include terms such as stock, debtors and cash.	☐	☐
9. Stock is a current asset and is shown on the profit and loss account.	☐	☐
10. Net margin is the same as return on sales.	☐	☐
11. Return on Investment (R.O.I.) is calculated by dividing gross profit by sales multiplied by 100.	☐	☐
12. Retained profit shown on the profit and loss account will result in a change in owners' equity on the balance sheet.	☐	☐
13. Reducing variable costs has the effect of increasing the contribution to fixed costs and profit.	☐	☐
14. Return on net assets can be calculated from the balance sheet alone.	☐	☐
15. Sales less working capital equals net current assets.	☐	☐
16. Contribution is gross profit less variable costs.	☐	☐
17. The bottom line is another name for working capital.	☐	☐
18. A cash flow forecast enables a company to estimate its projected receipts and expenditures.	☐	☐

19. Raw materials are usually classified as variable costs. ☐ ☐

20. The debtors' collection period indicates how quickly the debtors of a business are paying for their credit purchases. ☐ ☐

The correct answers can be found on the following pages.

Add up the total *correct* answers multiply by 5 = ... %

Answers to Final Test

Hopefully you did not need to guess this time round. Just in case you need a little help with one or two, we've included the brief explanation from the self assessment at the beginning of the book.

1. **False** The top line of the profit and loss account is Sales/Turnover/Revenue/Income.
2. **False** Working capital is the same as net *current* assets.
3. **True** The balance sheet is compiled at the end of an accounting period and shows the assets and liabilities at a 'frozen' moment in time.
4. **False** Assets of a business are made up of fixed and current assets. Current assets include stock, *debtors* and cash.
5. **True** The formula for cast of sales is: opening stock plus purchases less closing stock.
6. **True** Gross margin is gross profit expressed as a percentage of sales.
7. **False** The current ratio is a liquidity ratio and shows the relationship between the amount of money a company *owes* in the short-term (current liabilities) and how much it *owns* in the short-term (current assets). A ratio of 2:1 is considered healthy.
8. **False** Stock, debtors and cash are current assets, not current liabilities.
9. **False** Stock *is* a current asset but it is found on the balance sheet.
10. **True** They are interchangeable names. In both cases the formula is net profit divided by sales

multiplied by 100. In other words net profit expressed as a percentage of sales.

11. **False** The formula for Return on Investment is net profit divided by total assets multiplied by 100.

12. **True** Retained profit increases accumulated profit which goes to the balance sheet as reserves and is added to share capital. This increases owners' equity.

13. **True** The formula for contribution is sales less variable costs. Therefore, any reduction in variable costs will increase contribution. (In case you're wondering, contribution in this context goes towards fixed costs and thereafter profit.)

14. **False** You need the profit and loss account for the net profit and the balance sheet for the net assets.

15. **False** To begin with, working capital and net current assets are the same. Next, whereas sales is the top line of the profit and loss account, working capital or net current assets is a line on the balance sheet. Deducting one from the other serves no purpose. The calculation has no value whatsoever.

16. **False** Contribution is *sales* less variable costs.

17. **False** The bottom line refers to net profit before interest and tax.

18. **True** The cashflow statement is the budget expressed in terms of cash flowing into the business and cash flowing out.

19. **True** Any cost that varies in direct proportion to output is a variable cost.

20. **True** Debtors collection period or debtor days is an indication of the number of days it is taking for the company to collect money due.

Further reading

A. Rice (1999) *Accounts Demystified.* London: Financial Times Prentice Hall.

Paul McKoen and Leo Gough (1997) *The Finance Manual for Non-Financial Managers.* London: Pitman Publishing.

Roger Mason (1998) *Finance for Non-Financial Managers in a Week.* London: Hodder & Stoughton Educational.

Mark Allin (1997) *Painless Business Finance.* London: David Grant Publishing.

Further *Test Your …* titles from Hodder & Stoughton and the Institute of Management, all at £6.99

0 340 78006 1	Test Your Personality	❏
0 340 78050 9	Test Your Management Style	❏
0 340 78169 9	Test Your Management Skills	❏
0 340 78208 0	Test Your Leadership Skills	❏
0 340 78287 0	Test Your Financial Awareness	❏
0 340 78288 9	Test Your Literacy	❏
0 340 78290 0	Test Your Potential	❏

All Hodder & Stoughton books are available from your local bookshop or can be ordered direct from the publisher. Just tick the titles you want and fill in the form below. Prices and availability subject to change without notice.

To: Hodder & Stoughton Ltd, Cash Sales Department, Bookpoint, 78 Milton Park, Abingdon, Oxon OX14 4TD. If you have a credit card you may order by
telephone – 01235 400414
          fax – 01235 400454
E-mail address: orders@bookpoint.co.uk

Please enclose a cheque or postal order made payable to Bookpoint Ltd to the value of the cover price and allow the following for postage and packaging:

UK & BFPO: £4.30 for one book; £6.30 for two books; £8.30 for three books.

OVERSEAS & EIRE: £4.80 for one book; £7.10 for 2 or 3 books (surface mail).

Name: ....

Address: ....

....

....

If you would prefer to pay by credit card, please complete:

Please debit my Visa/Mastercard/Diner's Card/American Express (delete as appropriate) card no:

❏ ❏ ❏ ❏ ❏ ❏ ❏ ❏ ❏ ❏ ❏ ❏ ❏ ❏ ❏ ❏ ❏ ❏

Signature .... Expiry date ....

Further *Successful Business in a Week* **titles from Hodder & Stoughton and the Institute of Management all at £6.99**

All Hodder & Stoughton books are available from your local bookshop or can be ordered direct from the publisher. Just tick the titles you want and fill in the form below. Prices and availability subject to change without notice.

To: Hodder & Stoughton Ltd, Cash Sales Department, Bookpoint, 39 Milton Park, Abingdon, Oxon, OX14 4TD. If you have a credit card you may order by telephone – 01235 400414.

E-mail address: orders@bookpoint.co.uk

Please enclose a cheque or postal order made payable to Bookpoint Ltd to the value of the cover price and allow the following for postage and packaging:

UK & BFPO: £4.30 for one book; £6.30 for two books; £8.30 for three books.

OVERSEAS & EIRE: £4.80 for one book; £7.10 for 2 or 3 books (surface mail).

Name: ....

Address: ....

....

If you would prefer to pay by credit card, please complete:

Please debit my Visa/Mastercard/Diner's Card/American Express (delete as appropriate) card no:

❏❏❏❏❏❏❏❏❏❏❏❏❏❏❏❏❏❏

Signature .... Expiry Date ....